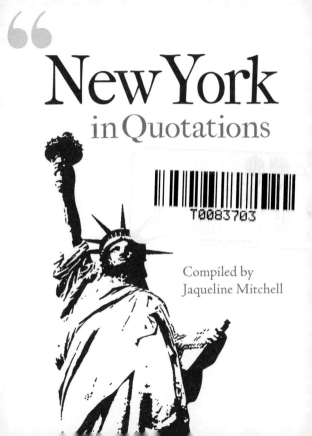

" New York
in Quotations

Compiled by
Jaqueline Mitchell

First published in 2016 by the
Bodleian Library
Broad Street
Oxford OX1 3BG
www.bodleianshop.co.uk

ISBN: 978 1 85124 420 1

All rights reserved. No part of this book may be reproduced,
stored in a retrieval system, or transmitted in any form or by
any means, electronic, mechanical, photocopying, recording,
or otherwise, without the written permission of the Bodleian
Library, except for the purpose of research or private study,
or criticism or review.

Selection and arrangement © Bodleian Library
Cover design by Dot Little
Designed and typeset by Rod Teasdale in 11 on 13pt Jenson
Printed and bound by L.E.G.O. spa, Vicenza

British Library Catalogue in Publishing Data
A CIP record of this publication is available from
the British Library

Oh mighty City of New York! you are
wonderful to behold, Your buildings are
magnificent, the truth be it told ...

William McGonagall,
Knight of the White
Elephant of Burmah
(1825–1902)

You will have heard of our taking of New Amsterdam... It did belong to England before, but the Dutch by degrees drove our people out and built a very good town, but we have got the better of it, and 'tis now called New York.

Charles II, king of England
(1630–1685)

The city seen from the Queensboro Bridge is always the city seen for the first time, in its first wild promise of all the mystery and the beauty in the world.

F. Scott Fitzgerald
(1896–1940)

> One could believe that giants had built this city for giants.

Ludwig Fulda
(1862–1939)

66

I love the city in an emotional, irrational way, like loving your mother or your father even though they're a drunk or a thief.

Woody Allen
(b. 1935)

99

The first thing that every English
visitor to New York notices is that
here everyone is his friend.

Quentin Crisp
(1908–1999)

I have seen next to nothing *grandiose*,
out of New York, in all our cities.
It makes 'em all look paltry and petty.

Oliver Wendell Holmes Sr
(1809–1894)

For most visitors to Manhattan, both foreign and domestic, New York is the Shrine of the Good Time.

Robert Benchley
(1889–1945)

"

I'm in love with New York. When you
bring your own riches to it, it is like
drinking from a Venetian glass. It is
beautiful, vital, and magical… It's
made for great swoops and daring and
for hope in life.

Anaïs Nin
(1903–1977)

New York, he supposed, was home –
the city of luxury and mystery, of
preposterous hopes and exotic dreams.

F. Scott Fitzgerald
(1896–1940)

It seemed almost intolerably shining, secure and well-dressed, as though it was continually going to gay parties while London had to stay home and do the housework.

Attributed to Noël Coward
(1899–1973)

"

New York is large, glamorous, easy-going, kindly and incurious – but above all it is a crucible – because it is large enough to be incurious.

Ford Madox Ford
(1873–1939)

"

Make your mark in New York and
you are a made man.

Mark Twain
(1835–1910)

Few commercial capitals have ever grown with more marvelous rapidity than New York. The great merchants and men of affairs who have built up her material prosperity, have not merely enriched themselves and their city; they have also played no inconsiderable part in the rapid opening up of the American continent during the present century, which has been rendered possible by the eagerness and far-reaching business ambition of commercial adventures, wielding the wonderful tools forged by the science of our day.

Theodore Roosevelt
(1858–1919)

New York attracts the most talented people in the world in the arts and professions. It also attracts them in other fields. Even the bums are talented.

Edmund Love
(1912–1990)

"

The inhabitants are in general brisk and
lively, kind to strangers, dress very gay,
the fair sex are in general handsome,
and said to be very obliging.

Patrick M'Robert
(fl. 1770s)

"

If there ever was an aviary over-stocked with jays it is that Yaptown-on-the-Hudson.

O. Henry
(William Sydney Porter)
(1862–1910)

"

Up in the heights of evening skies, my City of Cities float, in sunset's golden and crimson dyes: and a great joy clutches my throat.

James Oppenheim
(1882–1932)

"

Whoever is born in New York is
ill-equipped to deal with any other city:
all other cities seem, at best, a mistake,
and, at worst, a fraud.

James Baldwin
(1924–1987)

> New York, city of prose and fantasy, of capitalist automatism, its streets a triumph of cubism, its moral philosophy that of the dollar. New York impressed me tremendously because, more than any other city in the world, it is the fullest expression of our modern age.

Leon Trotsky
(1879–1940)

Cities give us collision. T'is said,
London and New York take the
nonsense out of a man.

Ralph Waldo Emerson
(1803–1882)

"

When New Yorkers tell one about the dangers of their city, the muggings, the dinner parties to which no-one turns up for fear of being attacked on the way, the traffic snarl-ups, the bland indifference of the city cops, they are unmistakably bragging.

Jonathan Raban
(b. 1942)

... the frankness, sincerity and generosity of this city, its hospitality without hidden motives and its eagerness to oblige and win approval, are simply astonishing and, at the same time, touching.

Pyotr Ilyich Tchaikovsky
(1840–1893)

"Dinner is New York's real function of the day.

Edward Hungerford
(1875–1948)

With the possible exception of London, there is no place like New York for versatility in eating and drinking.

J.G. Huneker
(1857–1921)

It couldn't have happened anywhere but in little old New York.

O. Henry
(William Sydney Porter)
(1862–1910)

It seemed, in spite of its irritating and noisy efficiency, a great and exciting place.

Noël Coward
(1899–1973)

66

… there is a good deal of fun about New York, if you only avoid fluster.

Walt Whitman
(1819–1892)

"As I drew near New York [City] I was first amused, and then somewhat staggered, by the cautious and grisly tales that went around. You would have thought we were to land upon a cannibal island.

Robert Louis Stevenson
(1850–1894)

“ New York is a different country. Maybe it ought to have a separate government. Everybody thinks differently, acts differently. They just don't know what the hell the rest of the United States is.

Henry Ford
(1863–1947)

New York... that unnatural city where every one is an exile, none more so than the American.

Charlotte Perkins Gilman
(1860–1935)

New York is the biggest collection of
villages in the world.

Alistair Cooke
(1908–2004)

New York is a cosmopolitan city; but it is not a city of cosmopolitans. Most of the masses in New York have a nation, whether or not it be the nation to which New York belongs.

Gilbert Keith Chesterton
(1874–1936)

The present in New York is so powerful
that the past is lost.

John Jay Chapman
(1862–1933)

The motorist whirs through the intersecting streets and round the corners, bent on suicide or homicide.

William Dean Howells
(1837–1920)

" ... we lingered in New York till the city felt so homelike that it seemed wrong to leave it. And further, the more one studied it, the more grotesque bad it grew.

Rudyard Kipling
(1865–1936)

> The City of Dreadful Height.

James Bone
(1872–1962)

New Yorkers temperamentally do not
crave comfort and convenience – if they
did they would live elsewhere.

E.B. White
(1899–1985)

> I'd forgotten how friendly the street people are in New York. In just a couple of hours six of them asked me if I was ok for change.

Bill Bryson
(b. 1951)

" New York is appalling, fantastically charmless and elaborately dire.

Henry James
(1843–1916)

… though one can dine in New York one could not dwell there.

Oscar Wilde
(1854–1900)

66

No one as yet has approached the management of New York in a proper spirit; that is to say, regarding it as the shiftless outcome of squalid barbarism and reckless extravagance.

Rudyard Kipling
(1865–1936)

New York is not a city where either life
or property is very secure.

Charles Mackay
(1814–1889)

"

A bulger of a place it is. The number of
ships beat me all hollow, and looked for
all the world like a big clearing in the
West, with the dead trees all standing.

David (Davy) Crockett,
(1786–1836)

"

The city drives me crazy, if you prefer, crazier; and I have no peace of mind or rest of body till I get out of it.

Lafcadio Hearn
(1850–1904)

How beautiful is this
Unmatched Cosmopolis!
City of wealth and want,
Of pitiless extremes,
Selfish ambitions, pure aspiring dreams.

Florence Coates
(1850–1927)

"

Everything there disappoints me but the crowd... It is a thousand times meaner than I could have imagined... The pigs in the street are the most respectable part of the population.

Henry David Thoreau
(1817–1862)

From this distance the city seems like a vast saw with black teeth. It breathes clods of black smoke into the sky and puffs like a glutton suffering from obesity.

Maxim Gorky
(1868–1936)

When they find themselves a little crowded, they simply tip a street on end and call it a sky-scraper.

William Archer
(1856–1924)

I like the rough impersonality of New York, where human relations are oiled by jokes, complaints, and confessions – all made with the assumption of never seeing the other person again.

Bill Bradley
(b. 1943)

... it is a splendid desert – a doomed and steepled solitude, where a stranger is lonely in the midst of a million of his race.

Mark Twain
(1835–1910)

With all the opulence and splendor of this city, there is very little good breeding to be found. We have been treated with an assiduous respect; and I have not seen one real gentleman, one well-bred man, since I came to town.

John Adams
(1735–1826)

"

That all one has to do to gather a large crowd in New York is to stand on the curb a few moments and gaze intently at the sky.

George Jean Nathan
(1882–1958)

"

... there seems to be some solvent in New York life that reduces all men to a common level, that touches everybody with its potent magic and brings to the surface the deeply underlying nobody.

William Dean Howells
(1837–1920)

… the people were all surprisingly rude and surprisingly kind.

Robert Louis Stevenson
(1850–1894)

Cities have sexes: London is a man,
Paris a woman, and New York a
well-adjusted transsexual.

Angela Carter
(1940–1992)

New York is a sucked orange.

Ralph Waldo Emerson
(1803–1882)

66

... this giant asparagus bed of alabaster and rose and green skyscrapers.

Cecil Beaton
(1904–1980)

To Europe she was America. To America she was the gateway to the earth. But to tell the story of New York would be to write a social history of the world.

H.G. Wells
(1866–1946)

They talk very fast, very loud, and altogether. They ask you a question, before you can utter three words of your answer, they will break out upon you again, and talk away.

John Adams
(1735–1826)

" … a walk through New York will disappoint an Englishman: there is, on the surface of society, a carelessness, a laziness, an unsocial indifference, which freezes the blood and disgusts the judgement.

Henry Bradshaw Fearon
(c.1770–1842)

"

" ... the art of getting ahead in New York was based on learning how to express dissatisfaction in an interesting way. The air was full of rage and complaint. People had no tolerance for your particular hardship unless you knew how to entertain them with it.

Don DeLillo
(b. 1936)

When I feel suicidal in Europe, it is mostly because of a sense of past failure – in art and human reactions alike. In New York such gloom rarely oppresses me: yesterday is dead.

Anthony Burgess
(1917–1993)

"New York is never dark and never quiet.

Paul Theroux
(b. 1941)

There is something in the New York
air that makes sleep useless.

Simone de Beauvoir
(1908–1986)

66

New York is Babylon: Brooklyn is the truly Holy City. New York is the city of envy, office work, and hustle; Brooklyn is the region of homes and happiness... There is no hope for New Yorkers, for they glory in their skyscraping sins; but in Brooklyn there is the wisdom of the lowly.

Christopher Morley
(1890–1957)

This is Broadway, the longest street with
the shortest memory.

Maurice Barrymore
(1849–1905)

"

I look out the window and I see the lights and the skyline and the people on the street rushing around looking for action, love, and the world's greatest chocolate chip cookie, and my heart does a little dance.

Nora Ephron
(1941–2012)

"

... in that city there is neurosis in the air which the inhabitants mistake for energy.

Evelyn Waugh
(1903–1966)

> I hate being rushed and hate New York
> because it is the city of haste.
>
> Christopher Isherwood
> (1904–1986)

66

Coming to New York from the muted mistiness of London, as I regularly do, is like travelling from a monochrome antique shop to a technicolor bazaar. … Manhattan is a place for coming and going; for raising up and pulling down; for making money and for spending it.

Kenneth Tynan
(1927–1980)

This narrow thoroughfare, baking and blistering in the sun, is Wall Street: the Stock Exchange and Lombard Street of New York. Many a rapid fortune has been made in this street, and many a no less rapid ruin.

Charles Dickens
(1812–1870)

Every man worships the dollar, and is down before his shrine from morning to night.

Anthony Trollope
(1815–1882)

"All men are alike in the U-nited States, an't they? It makes no odds whether a man has a thousand pound, or nothing, there. Particular in New York, I'm told.

Charles Dickens
(1812–1870)

The only trouble about this town is that it is too large. You cannot accomplish anything in the way of business, you cannot even pay a friendly call, without devoting a whole day to it.

Mark Twain
(1835–1910)

66

In Boston, they ask, How much does he know? In New York, How much is he worth?

Mark Twain
(1835–1910)

... the city of golden rewards

Sinclair Lewis
(1885–1951)

In New York you've got to have all the luck.

Charles Bukowski
(1920–1994)

I think New York one of the finest cities I ever saw... it rises like Venice, from the sea, and like that fairest of cities in the days of her glory, receives into its lap tribute of all the riches of the earth.

Frances Trollope
(1779–1863)

New York is my Lourdes. I go there for spiritual regeneration.

Brendan Behan
(1923–1964)

I have always said that New York was like heaven.

Quentin Crisp
(1908–1999)

When it's three o'clock in New York,
it's still 1938 in London.

Attributed to Bette Midler
(b. 1945)

66

New York, like London, seems to be
a cloacina of all the depravities of
human nature. New York is
appalling, fantastically charmless
and elaborately dire.

Thomas Jefferson
(1743–1826)

66

It was the old New York way... the way of people who dreaded scandal more than disease, who placed decency above courage, and who considered that nothing was more ill-bred than 'scenes', except the behaviour of those who gave rise to them.

Edith Wharton
(1862–1937)

The great characteristic of New York is din and excitement,—everything is done in a hurry—all is intense anxiety.

New York As It Is
(1863)

... beauty – a gift which, in the eyes of New York, justified every success, and excused a certain number of failings.

Edith Wharton
(1862–1937)

... but in my next transmigration, I think I should choose New York.

Ralph Waldo Emerson
(1803–1882)

Credits

The publisher gratefully thanks the many copyright holders below who have generously granted permission for the use of the quotations in this book. Every effort has been made to credit copyright holders of the quotations used in this book. We apologize for any unintentional omissions or errors and will insert the appropriate acknowledgement to any companies or individuals in the subsequent editions of the book.

p.1, William McGonagall, *Jottings of New York* (1890); p.2, Charles II, letter dated 24 October 1664; p.3, F. Scott Fitzgerald, reprinted with the permission of Scribner Publishing Group, a division of Simon & Schuster, Inc. from *The Great Gatsby* by F. Scott Fitzgerald. Copyright © 1925 by Charles Scribner's Sons. Copyright renewed © 1953 Frances Scott Fitzgerald Lanahan. All rights reserved; p.4, Ludwig Fulda, *Amerikanische Eindruke [American Impressions]* (1914); p.5, Woody Allen *Interviews* (2006) © Woody Allen, reprinted with the kind permission of Woody Allen, and University Press of Mississippi; p.6, © Estate of Quentin Crisp. Reprinted with the kind permission of the Quentin Crisp Estate c/o Radala & Associates; p.7, Oliver Wendell Holmes Sr, *The Professor at the Breakfast Table* (1860); p.8, © Estate of Robert Benchley. Used by permission of the Estate of Robert Benchley, Nat Benchley, Executor; p.9, excerpt from *A Literate Passion* by Anais Nin and Henry Miller. Copyright © 1987 by Rupert Pole, as Trustee under the Last Will and Testament of Anais Nin. Reprinted by permission of Houghton Mifflin Harcourt Publishing Company. All rights reserved; p.10, with the permission of Scribner Publishing Group, a division of Simon & Schuster, Inc. from *The Beautiful and the Damned* by F. Scott Fitzgerald. Copyright © 1922 by Charles Scribner's Sons. Copyright renewed © 1950 by Frances Scott Fitzgerald Lanahan. All rights reserved; p.11, attributed to Noël Coward, reprinted with the kind permission of the Noël Coward Estate; p.12, Ford Madox Ford, from

'My Gotham' (1927); p.13, *Mark Twain's Notebooks and Journals*, Vol. 1: *1855 -73* ; p.14, Theodore Roosevelt, *New York, 1890-5* (1895); p.15, © 1956, 1957 by Edmund G. Love, permission granted, Blanche C. Gregory Inc., New York, NY; p.16, Patrick M'Robert, *A Tour through Part of the North Provinces of America in the Years 1774 & 1775* (reprinted 1935); p.17, O. Henry, *The Gentle Grafter* (1908); p.18, James Oppenheim, *Songs for the New Age* (1914); p.19, James Baldwin, *Just above my Head*, (1979); p.20, Leon Trotsky, *My Life* (1930); p.21, Ralph Waldo Emerson, *The Conduct of Life* (1872); p.22, © Jonathan Raban, *Soft City* (1974); p.23, *The Diaries of Tchaikovsky* (1945) ; p.24, Edward Hungerford, *The Personality of American Cities* (1913); p.25, J.G. Huneker, *New Cosmopolis* (1915); p.26, O. Henry, *A Little Local Colour* (1910); p.27, © Noël Coward Estate; p.28, Walt Whitman, *Complete Prose Works* (1901); p.29, Robert Louis Stevenson, *The Amateur Emigrant* (1905); p.30, Henry Ford, from *Reader's Digest*, October 1973 © Reader's Digest; p.31, *The Living of Charlotte Perkins Gilman, An Autobiography* (1935); p.32, © Alistair Cooke Estate; p.33, G.K. Chesterton, *What I Saw in America* (1922) ; p.34, from *John Jay Chapman and His Letters*, ed. M.A.de Wolfe Howe (1937); p.35, © Harper's Magazine Foundation; p.36, Rudyard Kipling, *Letters of Travel, 1892-1913* (1920); p.37, James Bone, reprinted with kind permission of Pushcart Press; p.38, © Estate of E.B. White; p.39, © Bill Bryson, reprinted with kind permission February 2016; p.40, Henry James, *The Letters of Henry James* (1920); p.41, Oscar Wilde, 'The American Invasion' (1887); p.42, Rudyard Kipling, *Letters of Travel* (1920) ; p.43, Charles Mackay, *Life and Liberty in America* (1859); p.44, Davy Crockett, *An Account of Col. Crockett's Tour to the North* (1835); p.45, *Life and Letters of Lafcadio Hearn*, ed. by Elisabeth Bisland (1906); p.46, Florence Coates, *The Book of New York's Verse* (1917); p.47, H.D. Thoreau, *The Atlantic Monthly* (1892); p.48, Maxim Gorky, *Appleton's Magazine*, Vol. 8 (1906); p.49, William Archer, from *America Today* (1900); p.50, © Bill Bradley. From *Life on the Run* (1976); p.51, Mark Twain, *Alta California*, letter dated 5 June 1867; p.52, *The Works of John Adams* (1850); p.53, © The George Jean Nathan Estate, granted with permission of Patricia Angelini; p.54, W.D. Howells, *A Hazard of New Fortunes* (1889); p.55, Robert Louis Stevenson, *Essays of Travel* (1905); p.56, *Shaking a Leg: Collected Journalism and Writings*, by Angela Carter.

Published by Chatto & Windus, 1997. Copyright ©Angela Carter.
Reproduced by permission of the Estate of Angela Carter c/o Rogers,
Coleridge & White Ltd., Powis Mews, London W11 1JN; p.57, Ralph
Waldo Emerson, *The Conduct of Life* (1861); p.58 © Literary Executor of
the late Sir Cecil Beaton and Rupert Crew Limited; p.59, H.G. Wells,
The War in the Air (1908); p.60, *The Works of John Adams* (1850); p.61,
H.B. Fearon, *Sketches of America* (1819); p.62, © Don DeLillo, reprinted
by permission of Macmillan Publishers. From *White Noise* (1984); p.63,
© International Anthony Burgess Foundation. From *New York* (1977);
p.64, Paul Theroux, *My Other Life* (1996) © Cape Cod Scriveners Co.
1996, used by permission of The Wylie Agency (UK) Limited; p.65,
America Day by Day, translated by Carol Cosman, © 1999 by the
Regents of the University of California, published by the University of
California Press. Translated from the original *L'Amérique au jour le jour*,
Simone de Beauvoir © Éditions Gallimard (1954); p.66, Christopher
Morley, *Parnassus on Wheels* (1917); p.68, *Heartburn* (1983) © Estate of
Nora Ephron; p.69, *Brideshead Revisited* © 1945 Evelyn Waugh; p.70,
Liberation Diaries, © Don Bachardy, 2012, reprinted by permission of
HarperCollins Publishers and used by permission of The Wylie Agency
(UK) Limited; p.71, *Tynan Right and Left* (1967) © Estate of Kenneth
Tynan, reprinted with the kind permission of Roxana and Matthew
Tynan; p. 72, © Estate of Charles Dickens, reprinted with the kind
permission of Commander Mark Dickens; p.73, reprinted with the
approval of A.S. Trollope; p.74, © Estate of Charles Dickens, reprinted
with the kind permission of Commander Mark Dickens; p.75, Mark
Twain, *Daily Alta California* (1867); p.76, Mark Twain, *North America
Review* (1895); p.77, Sinclair Lewis, *The Job: An American Novel* (1917) ;
p.78, © Estate of Charles Bukowski, reprinted with the kind permission
of Mrs Linda Lee Bukowski; p.79, reprinted with the approval of A.S.
Trollope; p.80, © The Brendan Behan Estate; p.81, © Estate of Quentin
Crisp. Reprinted with the kind permission of the Quentin Crisp Estate
c/o Radala & Associates; p.82, Bette Midler, quoted in the London
Times, 21 September 1978; p.83, Thomas Jefferson, letter dated 8
September 1823; p.84, Edith Wharton, *The Age of Innocence* (1920); p. 85,
New York As It Is (1863); p.86, Edith Wharton, *The Age of Innocence*
(1920); p.87, Ralph Waldo Emerson, letter dated 1842.